Twenty Keys to Success

Deborah Carpenter

ISBN: 978-0-6151-6080-1

TABLE OF CONTENTS

Chapter One   1

Chapter Two   3

Chapter Three   7

Chapter Four   10

Chapter Five   11

Chapter Six   13

Chapter Seven   15

Chapter Eight   16

Chapter Nine   19

Chapter Ten   20

Chapter Eleven   21

Chapter Twelve   22

Chapter Thirteen   23

Chapter Fourteen   25

Chapter Fifteen   26

Chapter Sixteen   27

Chapter Seventeen   28

Chapter Eighteen   29

Chapter Nineteen   30

Chapter Twenty   32

ACKNOWLEDGEMENTS

I would like to thank my parents for their kindness and generosity.

FORWARD

Dear Reader,

I have endeavored to make the writing style in this book as straight forward and as easy to understand as possible. I have also tried to avoid "religion" (although some may disagree with me). My reference point and base of experience is my Christian faith. Nevertheless, the spiritual truths contained herein are applicable to the Christian and to any other individual who chooses to apply them. The Good Lord or as some would call the Spirit loves us all, and we can all benefit from His love and goodness if we choose. Apply these truths to your life and be blessed with Health, Happiness, Success and Perfect Self-Expression. He loves you, and that is what He wants for you.

TWENTY KEYS TO SUCCESS...

How do you win at the game of life?

Don't play desperately, don't play scared, play to win, believe that you will win, stop worrying, and keep believing!

Have you ever wondered why the rich get richer and the poor get poorer?

Those that feel "entitled" always seem to get what they want!

Good things always seem to happen to happy people and tragedy and crisis always seem to follow some individuals.

Why is this? How can you have the good things in life come to you?

The Lord has *already* given us all things that pertain to life and godliness. II Peter 1:3

My God shall supply all of your needs according to His riches in glory. Philippians 4:19

I came that ye might have life and have it more abundantly. John 10:10

Jesus, though He was rich, yet He became poor for our sakes so that we might become rich. II Corinthians 8:9

When the word "rich" in this passage is looked up in Strong's Concordance the translation given is material wealth.

Does this sound like you are supposed to have health and be blessed financially?

So how do these blessings become manifested in your life?

The blessings and promises of the Lord don't fall on us like ripe fruit off a tree. They are appropriated by faith.

Theories of quantum physics have shown that electrons exist in a state of "possibility", until someone looks at them and they become the expected result.

This book contains "Twenty Keys to Success" for every area of your life.

CHAPTER 1

1. For as a man thinketh in his heart, so is he. Proverbs 23:7

Your thought is a creative power. You are the creator of your own reality, not a victim of circumstance. You choose your thoughts and the Spirit of God helps to bring those thoughts to pass.

The things that you think about will materialize into your life. Think back over your life, how many things that have happened had you thought about or visualized before they came to pass? Thoughts produce things, sometimes it is called the Law of Attraction, and Jesus said you reap what you sow. The thoughts you send out are what you get back. This works for material things and for spiritual and emotional results as well. So whatever thoughts you are thinking, you better make sure they are in your size!

Thought or desire is a powerful magnet that draws things or people or events to you. These could be the desires of your heart or the things that you fear. Job said "that which I greatly feared has come upon me." [1] His thoughts of fear left an access point for the events that followed. The Universe or the Almighty wants to give you whatever you ask for. Whatever you focus your thoughts on consistently, either good or bad, will become manifest in your life.

---

[1] Job 3:25 KJV

Theories of Quantum Physics state that electrons exist in the form of a cloud or a state of "possibility" until they are observed. At that time the electrons take the form of whatever result the observer is expecting (thinking). Those electrons are waiting for you to give them form, by faith and thought.

Good things happen to happy people because they draw the good to themselves by their happy and optimistic thoughts. The people who act "entitled" always get what they feel/think/believe they are entitled to.

It's all good! Expect a good outcome from every situation and it will become good. All things work together for good to those who love the Lord and are called according to His purposes.[2] "Whatsoever things are of good report; if there be any virtue, if there be any praise, think on these things."[3]

---

[2] Romans 8:28 KJV
[3] Philippians 4:8 KJV

CHAPTER 2

2. Meditation brings manifestation.

Spend time each day meditating on your desired outcome or manifestation. The more that you meditate the more faith will be developed for the manifestation to come. Meditation builds your faith and brings substance to what you believe for. Faith is the substance of things hoped for and the evidence of things not seen.[4] Faith is the bridge that brings the desires of your heart, the answers to your prayers, into this physical world. Faith is developed by meditation because you hear yourself say something over and over. Faith comes by hearing.[5]

Affirmations are meditation.

Meditate using scripture verses and other phrases that relate to your manifested desires. Repeat these over and over to yourself, these are your affirmations. Say them until they become real to your inner man. Then keep on saying them out loud or just to yourself, silently. If you get to the point where you believe inside yourself and don't doubt in your heart, then you will have whatever you say.[6] Continue to meditate like this and the answer to your prayer will seem as though it becomes real right in front of you, then reach out and take it. Your manifestation will arrive shortly thereafter.

---

[4] Hebrews 11:1 KJV
[5] Romans 10:17 KJV
[6] Mark 11:23-24 KJV

Write down the vision and make it plain.

Write the vision and make it plain (clear, easy to understand) upon the tables so that he may run that readeth it.[7]

When you write down your dreams, desires and goals it impresses them upon your spirit and the Spirit of God. The greater one lives in you, He is waiting to hear from you. Writing things down repeatedly helps in your concentration and focus. It helps you to see your goals in the spirit realm and bring them into manifestation by developing your faith. Each time you write something down it gets stronger and stronger in your spirit until it has become "substance" on the inside.

Each day spend time writing down a clear detailed description of your dreams. Make it as clear and specific as you can, this gives the Spirit of God something to work with. Write this down in a notebook as many times as you can each day until you know in your spirit that you have it. This is a type of meditation also and will build your faith.

Start a folder of pictures or a "vision board".

Find pictures that represent your goals and dreams. Keep them in a folder or make up a board of all of them together. This will help keep your thoughts and imaginations focused. Focus is important, like burning paper through a magnifying glass.

---

[7] Habakkuk 2:2 KJV

Study your folder each morning in the quiet time when you just wake up before your mind is cluttered with the concerns of the day. Or study the folder or vision board at night before you retire and thank the Lord for all of the things that you see. Develop scenarios around the pictures of how you will be enjoying all of them when they come. Keep doing this or all of these meditations until you have your manifested answers.

When you do your visualizing try to make it so that you actually *feel* as though you are there enjoying having the things. When feeling is applied it speeds up the development of the manifestation. It helps to make your faith more real and makes things develop more quickly because the Spirit has more to work with. Faith is developed the more that you meditate and visualize. That is when faith is the substance of things hoped for and the evidence of things not seen.[8] This is where the seeds of your faith (desires of your heart) are conceived and develop into reality. Nurture these seeds with your continued meditations, visualizations, affirmations and gratitude daily. Meditate with your writing, folders, vision boards and affirmations every day. Bring yourself to a place in your imagination where you are feeling and enjoying the answers to your prayers. Then bring yourself to a place of gratitude, then release it all to the Spirit and know that it is done.

Meditate on the fact that you already have in your possession the desired result now. You actually do have it; it just hasn't materialized in this world yet. If you believe that you will have it later, that is when you will have it ...later, and later

---

[8] Hebrews 11:1 KJV

and later. The spirit world takes your requests literally. State that you have your answer now, because you do.

The more clear our visualizations the greater vitality we put into our "seeds", the quicker they will germinate. Any anxious thoughts, or pressure or despair, or giving up (doubt) will cause a reversal of this process. The father of a child said "Lord I believe, help thou my unbelief."[9] The Spirit will help you if you ask. Water your seeds of faith by quietly meditating on your desires as accomplished facts. This will keep the doubt at bay. Trust in the creative power of the Lord to do the rest.

Be careful how you ask, never say "I want". Remember the spirit world is very literal. If you say "I want" you will wind up in a state of wanting. Remember "the Lord is my Shepherd, I shall not want."[10]

Keep things in the now, in the dimension of the Spirit there is no time or space so all things are now, your prayers are answered when you ask. That is why the Lord is the Great I Am, the Great Lord of Now.

---

[9] Mark 9:24 KJV
[10] Psalm 23:1 KJV

CHAPTER 3

3. Planting the seed and watering the seed.

To apply the creative power of thought you need to consider the thing as done and that it is already in existence in the unseen dimension. This is the seed that you have conceived. Jesus said that if you have believed that you have received the thing then you have it.[11] When you think this way you are assured that your seed will invariably and infallibly bear fruit. At that point if you hold your focus on the goal steady and keep the thought that the thing is done then that thought becomes its own center of attraction for all that is necessary for its creation.

Once you have conceived the seed inside yourself, or you know that you have faith for your desired manifestation or answer, the seed of faith that you have conceived needs to be nurtured. You water the seed with your affirmation and meditations. The more watering, the quicker the growth. The more praise, the more thanks, the more gratitude, the sooner the manifestation. Praise, thanksgiving, and gratitude water the seeds of faith.

You may see a partial manifestation or a "blade" spring up. Keep watering the seed, now is not the time to stop. Partial manifestation is like the little sprouts of a new plant. Remember "first the blade, then the ear, then the full corn in the ear"[12] then comes the harvest.

---

[11] Mark 11:24 KJV
[12] Mark 4:28 KJV

Worry, doubt, fear, unbelief, anger, resentment, jealousy, unforgiveness, or any other negative emotion will choke out the seeds of faith so that they will be unable to bear fruit for you.[13]   Faith works in an atmosphere of love.[14]   Love, happiness, and gratitude keep the channels of faith and blessing open. **No whining! No complaining! No gossip!** These things are like taking poison and will block all the channels of blessing. When you find yourself in a negative mindset, meditate on the fact that the Lord is good, and that He is good to you. This will bring His goodness on the scene. He is goodness. He is the Healer and the healing, the Giver and the gift.

Some days you may struggle to remain positive and maintain a positive confession. Try not to speak anything negative. Some days might not be as perfectly positive as we would like them to be. Guess what? You are human just like the rest of us. Pick up the pieces the next day, get back into your meditations and affirmations and continue on. It helps to support your spirit with reading or listening to positive material.

Sometimes it is hard to do on your own. Find a friend who will believe with you and support you.

Where two of you agree on earth as touching anything they shall ask, it shall be done for them of my Father in heaven.[15]

Every day has the seeds of success in it but on some days it can be harder to see. Thank the Lord for your success,

---

[13] Mark 4:19
[14] Galatians 5:6
[15] Matthew 18:19

8

healing, etc. and move on to the next day. You don't need to ask a second time, He heard the first time, just hang in there, it's on the way! When you ask the second time it's as if you are starting over. If you need to, you can ask until you know in your spirit that you have it, and then go from there. Walk by your faith and not by what you see. This takes some discipline of your thought life at first, but it gets easier as you practice it.

When you first start to do this, for a while your circumstances won't look any different. Start to see yourself as different on the inside and before long the change on the inside will begin to change what is on the outside.

It may be frustrating at first experiencing the "I have, I don't have" tug of war going on in your mind. Just keep going, until it becomes normal to think "I have it!" without seeing it. Even if you don't get perfect results every time, don't worry, it's the intention that impresses the Spirit.

There is the "shake out" period when everything looks like its all going wrong. Ignore this; don't talk about how bad things are or how bad things look. Keep your mind and heart on the positive outcome you are expecting. The Almighty is bigger than the problem that you face. He will give you the victory if you give Him your faith and trust. Remember, your thought is a creative power. You and the Spirit are co-creators.

CHAPTER 4

4. Expect the unexpected good, expect supernatural answers and help.

The Almighty is a supernatural God who works outside of our dimension. Keep your eye on Him not the situation. He is able when we are not. That is what He is there for! All things are possible for he who believes in a supernatural God.

Things are impossible for man but nothing is impossible with God.[16]

The Lord works outside of natural law:

He causes axe heads to swim. II Kings 6:6
He turns water to wine. John 2:9
He makes the sun to stand still in Gibeon and the moon in Ajalon. Joshua 10:13
He multiplies the loaves and fishes. Matthew 14:19
He answers by fire. I Kings 18:38
He parts the great waters. Exodus 14:22, Joshua 3:16
He raises the dead. John 11:43
He reverses time. Isaiah 38:8
And many more!

---

[16] Mark 10:27 paraphrase KJV

CHAPTER 5

5. Praise and Thanksgiving, and Gratitude

The more that you give praise and thanksgiving for the answer to your prayer the sooner the manifestations will appear. This is also part of meditation and will keep the seeds of your faith growing.

Thank the Lord for the perfect answer to your prayers. You can get a counterfeit if you don't specify a perfect answer. The devil can disguise himself as an angel of light. Just because something looks like your opportunity doesn't mean that it is.

Tell the Lord that He is good, and thank Him for His goodness. This brings good things into your life because it brings Him on the scene. He likes it when he hears you say good things about Him. Wouldn't you?

When you can't focus on the desired outcome, meditate on the Lord's goodness; be grateful and thankful to Him because He is good. When you meditate on His goodness it brings all that He is into your situation. That's because He inhabits the praises of His people.[17] Make a list of all that you are grateful for and guess what it will bring, more of that same goodness, and more to be thankful for. Remember the 23rd Psalm, "surely goodness and mercy shall follow me all the days of my life".

---

[17] Psalm 22:3

Make songs and melodies in your heart of thanksgiving to the Lord.[18] Sing to the Lord as you go through your day (you can sing silently too). Song is a very powerful spiritual tool. Thank the Lord that you already have your heart's desire, because you do. As soon as you prayed, He answered. In the place where there is no time and space the answer to your prayer already exists. Faith is the bridge that will bring substance to it and bring it into this world.

---

[18] Ephesians 5:19

CHAPTER 6

6. Don't push or force the issue, remain "indifferent" and relaxed.

The force of our own will can obtain some things also. This is manipulation and witchcraft and the results won't be happy or satisfactory, the results won't be perfect. The force of our own will can bring us into the spiritual world also, but there are other spirits or entities there that will affect the outcome of what happens. Unless we go with the armor of love and goodness we are not protected there. When you push too hard you will get what you are going after but something will be wrong with it. Instead hold the desires of your heart, in your heart with love and tenderness. Every good and perfect gift comes from the Father. There is a delicate balance between standing in faith, believing the Lord will work things out for you, and pushing using the force of your own will. If it feels like you are pushing, or pushing against a wall, you are. You don't have to push to obtain things from a loving Father; just enter into a place of rest. He wants you to have the things you asked for. Ask the Spirit to give you wisdom in knowing what to do. He may be saying not now or redirecting you. (If you believe for a healing He wants you healed now or as soon as your faith is developed enough to receive it).

Cast all of your cares upon the Lord as far as they concern the answer to prayer. Hold your desires in a place of love in the midst of your heart. Think of them tenderly and lovingly all during the day. You don't need to push or force, just surround your wishes, desires, and goals with love, joy and happiness. Thank the Lord that your prayers are being answered in His perfect way.

Remain "indifferent", if you desire something intensely or are very impatient for a manifestation, that is really worry and fear in disguise. Worry blocks your desires from coming to pass. The Spirit needs a relaxed and happy person to work through. Stay happy and light; this keeps your channels open to receive your blessings. Watch funny movies, smile and stay away from negative people. Cast your concerns on the Lord, release the matter to Him and know that He has heard and answered your prayer. His answer is always yes if your prayer lines up with His will and goodness.

You can only expect the results that your heart truly wants. There is no fooling the Spirit. You can't expect success at a job that you really don't want to do. You will resent the job and no matter how much you are standing in faith for a positive outcome it will only go so far because you really want to be somewhere else. Ask the Spirit to put you in the perfect place for you, the place where you were divinely meant to be.

CHAPTER 7

7. Ask correctly.

Your prayers for someone else won't be effective if the person isn't in agreement with you. Regardless of how much faith you may have, you can't override someone else's will. It is the same thing as witchcraft to try to dominate or manipulate someone else.

Ask that your prayers be answered in the Lord's perfect way. Ask that all that is yours by divine plan and design come to you in a perfect way through faith and by His grace.

Be as specific as possible when making your requests to the Spirit. Always thank Him for the answer.

CHAPTER 8

8. Timing

Take your hands off the situation, don't try to manipulate or force things to happen because they will turn out wrong. Manipulating or forcing gets in the way of the Spirit and His way of doing things. Don't try to figure out how things will transpire because this will slow things down. The Spirit will work things out in a way you never thought of. You don't need to know how it will work out, you probably would mess it up if you did. Loose the situation into the hand of the Almighty for Him to work out. Cast your care on the Lord, for He cares for you.

He can't do anything until you take your hands off the situation. He is able to keep the things that we commit to Him, but we have to let go of the problem or situation and truly commit it to him. Many manifestations can come immediately when you truly let go. This is why sometimes when you give up, the answer comes right away. Enter in to His rest and don't take the situation back, don't ask a second time, that is just spinning your wheels. Jesus said that the kingdom of heaven is like a field where the farmer sows the seeds and lies down and sleeps and while he is sleeping the seed springs up and he doesn't know how it happened.[19] In other words when you sow your seed of faith or make an offering towards your goal, don't worry about how it is going to come up, don't worry about how it will all happen, it just will, because that's what seeds do.

---

[19] Mark 4:27

State your affirmations and meditations knowing that you have received the answer or desired result now. Now is the day of your salvation.[20]

Your answers will become manifested when your spirit is fully convinced that it has the answers now. That is what meditation accomplishes; it develops faith in your spirit and then becomes substance in the spirit world and in this world.

When you have learned how to use your faith some prayers will come to pass right away. Jesus never said that we had to wait; He healed most people immediately or shortly thereafter.

After years of looking at the glass as half empty it may take time to turn your thought processes around to a positive direction, but it can be done if you stay with it. It can be discouraging when you don't see changes right away but don't let yourself stay in that frame of mind. To everything there is a season. It takes a season for a plant to develop from a seed. Your faith is a seed and it will take time for the seed to develop to a full harvest (your answer).

Try not to be hard on yourself. It takes time for things to change. Things have to change on the inside of you before they change on the outside. Eventually you learn new habits of thought and it becomes easier. Don't condemn yourself that is self defeating. Never be impatient when you don't succeed at every try. It is your intention that counts, not necessarily absolute fulfillment every time. The Spirit understands, He is the all knowing power, He knows what is

---

[20] II Corinthians 6:2

in your heart and will reward accordingly. Be diligent and patient and you will succeed.

Remember the more time you spend on meditation, affirmation, and writing in your notebook, and on praise and thanksgiving, the more quickly your faith is developed and the sooner your answer arrives. This works in reverse also, the more complaining and condemning, criticizing and judging, the longer a bad situation will stay around. The more you fight and resist a situation the longer it will persist, because you are putting energy into thinking about it.

If you quit talking about adverse situations they will disappear on their own. Some situations can be very difficult, but don't talk about them with everyone over and over again. If you have to talk about it say it one time, say everything you need to say, and then let it go. Try not to think about the situation either, don't give it any attention. If you can take your mind off it, the problem will just dry up and go away.

Please note if you find yourself in an abusive situation, don't wait for it to go away. Don't in any situation, put yourself in danger, leave and get to a safe place. Then start to believe for better things.

CHAPTER 9

9. The Lord wants you to have happiness, health and success. Do you believe that?

He who already gave us His only son, how much more will He not give good things to them that ask Him?[21]

Jesus though He was rich, became poor for our sakes that we might become rich.[22]

Beloved I wish above all things that you would prosper and be in good health even as your soul prospers.[23]

Trust in the living God who gave us all things richly to enjoy.[24]

---

[21] Matthew 7:11 KJV
[22] II Corinthians 8:9 KJV
[23] II John 1:2 KJV
[24] I Timothy 6:7 KJV

CHAPTER 10

10. Is your heart condemning you? Is the adversary condemning you?

If our heart condemns us not then we know that we have the things that we ask of Him.[25] Is there someone who you need to forgive? Jesus said that when you stand praying (asking) forgive, that means forgive yourself also, He already has. Forgiveness can set you free from a prison of pain, anger or loneliness and depression, or sickness. Forgiveness is healing, and it opens the channels of your blessing. Unforgiveness will block your blessings.

Is the Adversary condemning you? Are you experiencing or hearing thoughts of insecurity, inadequacy, condemnation, self hate, or feeling undeserving? There is therefore now no condemnation to those who are in Christ Jesus.[26] He says that you don't have to accept those judgments and condemnations! *Not every voice that you hear in your head is your voice or your thought.* You get to decide what gets to stay in your mind, don't let the negative thought stay there and make a home. Meditate on your positive affirmations and the word of the Lord. Meditate on my word day and night and you shall make thy way prosperous and have good success.[27] Whatever is good and perfect and of good report, think on these things.[28]For as a man thinketh in his heart, so is he.[29]

---

[25] I John 3:20
[26] Romans 8:1
[27] Joshua 1:8
[28] Philippians 4:8
[29] Proverbs 23:7

20

CHAPTER 11

11. Movies, television, friends, books, the internet.

Are these positive influences? Be careful with who you share your confidences and conversation. The things that you hear will influence your thought life if you are not careful. Don't spend time with complainers, whiners or gossips, these influences are poisonous to your life and blessing.

CHAPTER 12

12. Watch over your thought life and what you say.

What you are not giving your attention to (in **your** life) will be influenced by what others are saying and thinking about your situation. Your life will be influenced by what others say and think about your life and affairs by default. Make sure that your life and family are covered by positive thoughts and words. Be cautious about who you share your thoughts with. Make sure those you have told will speak positive words in regards to you and your life and affairs.

CHAPTER 13

13. Being double minded.

Everything within you, your mind, spirit and heart all need to be in agreement on what ever it is that you want to see come to pass. Every part of you must desire the same outcome or you will see very little or no results. You will be stuck going around the same mountain again and again. If your heart wants things one way but your mind wants it another guess who wins out? It's like one step forward, two steps back. You can't fake out the Spirit.

Think of your innermost desires as an accomplished fact. You cannot think positive and negative thoughts at the same time. This is what Jesus called being double minded. He said that a double minded man is unstable in all his ways and would not (could not) receive anything from the Lord.[30] You need to stay on track to give the Spirit a chance to finish His work.

You are the one who decides what thoughts, feelings and ideas get to stay in your mind. You can control your thoughts by an act of your will. Your will is what keeps you focused, it keeps your thoughts going in the right direction. Sometimes it can be a struggle, that's o.k.; you are developing new muscles, keep working on it!

When you need to strengthen your faith or resolve ask the Holy Spirit to help you. "Lord I believe, help thou my

---

[30] James 1:7

unbelief." It's o.k. to ask for help, "You have not because you ask not, ask that you may receive that your joy may be full."[31] He will help; He is your Helper and your Comforter, a friend that sticks closer than a brother. Jesus is the author and the finisher of your faith.[32]

---

[31] John 16:24
[32] Hebrews 12:2 KJV

CHAPTER 14

14. The Law of Attraction works in reverse also.

When you complain, gossip, or speak negatively about your job, relationship, or a situation you are currently in, or anything, you are really cursing yourself. If you believe and don't doubt in your heart, you will have **whatever** you say, good or bad! Asking "Why God why?" Or "When God when?" is really whining, or just worry and fear in disguise. Don't complain or condemn the moment or situation that you find yourself in, don't be impatient, this will put you in a position of fear and wanting and will only delay or block the answers or manifestations you are looking for. Complaining will only make the situations worse or make them stick around longer and you will get more of what you are complaining about!

Don't condemn the situation or the place that you are in. Ask that it become a blessing to you somehow. Ask for wisdom so that you may learn from the situation so that you may go on. Ask for the grace and strength to get through the season or place that you are in. As you bless the place or situation you will reap what you sow. One more mention, that if you are in a dangerous or abusive situation it is not the time to stay and ask for a blessing. Get out, and then ask for the help and blessings.

CHAPTER 15

15. It takes a lot of physical energy and stamina to constantly stay positive.

Take care of yourself physically. Make sure you eat a healthy diet and get rest. It can be very difficult to stay positive when you are sick, tired or depressed. Exercise and take walks, take your vitamins and if you need medical help of any sort or medication for depression please take it.

In the beginning it is easier to start out on small projects because you are still learning how to use your faith. If however, you need something big like getting a big bill paid off, start out way in advance of the due date to give your faith time to grow.

CHAPTER 16

16. Concentration

Staying focused is very important because it focuses the creative energy of your thought like burning paper with a magnifying glass. You can't make an affirmation here and there and make progress. You can't just float; you need to stay engaged in the process. A good exercise to help develop concentration is to say "Thank you Lord for wealth, health, beauty, love and success" (or whatever your project is). Say this over and over and count on one finger each time that you repeat it. Go through all fingers and do it ten times. It is good to say it silently as you go to sleep at night or first thing in the morning.

CHAPTER 17

17. The will of God.

He is an expansive creator of life and He seeks to find that creative expression in you and through you. Does it make sense that the One who created beauty, love and goodness would seek expression in things that are the opposite? How do things such as sickness, depression, and poverty correspond with a loving Creator who already gave His best for you? He needs you for His self expression the way a husband needs a wife and a bridegroom needs a bride. He desires that you would be that perfect expression of Himself through you. This only happens through a loving, relaxed, happy vessel. How he chooses to express Himself is different and creative in every one of us, because He is infinitely different and creative. Trust that the good things that you desire, the visions that He has flashed across your imagination, the ones that you thought were too good to be true, are really His divine will and direction for your life.

CHAPTER 18

18. Healing

The basis of all healing is a change in belief. Whatever our mind creates is a reflection of that belief. A belief which has been ingrained from childhood cannot be turned around or changed at a moments notice. This is why sometimes after prayer there is improvement but after a while the symptoms return. Whatever our conception of the Lord is, that is what He will become to us. He is bound by the laws that He created. If we regard Him as a benevolent power, supplying our needs and healing us, that allows Him to do those things.

CHAPTER 19

19. Speak to your mountain.

Say over and over in your mind as you go to sleep "health, happiness, prosperity". The Spirit hears your silent prayers and affirmations as well. Call your money, health, etc. to come to you. Speak to the north, the south, the east and the west, say that all that is divinely appointed as yours comes to you now. Declare that what the Lord has given to you comes to you now in a perfect way. We have been given authority in this earth to declare things as we would like them to be.[33] The Spirit responds by answering your prayers, desires of your heart, and declarations when we do them in faith. Do these until you see the results.

Jesus said we could speak to the mountain and tell it to go.[34] Then it stands to reason that the converse is true, you can speak to the things you desire and call them, and they would come to you. Call those things in your life that be not as though they are, saying they are in your life right now.[35] If we can tell the mountain that it has to go then we can speak to things like jobs, homes, cars, perfect relationships, healing, etc. and tell them to come to us. The Lord has given us all things richly to enjoy.[36] The Lord told Ezekiel to speak to the valley of dry bones and call them to arise and take on flesh. He told Ezekiel to speak to the mountains, hills, valleys and streams and to call the Spirit to come and breathe

---

[33] Job 22:23
[34] Matthew 21:21
[35] Romans 4:17
[36] I Timothy 6:17

life into the slain that they would live.[37]   Are you speaking life or death into your situations?   Call every Lazarus that looks dead (career, relationship, healing) in your life to be raised up.   The power of life and death is in the tongue.[38] What are you saying?

There is a popular teaching called "name it and claim it". This idea springs from spiritual truth but is incomplete without total alignment of mind and heart. Jesus said that "if you believe and don't doubt in your heart, you would have whatever you say."   In other words, if you believe in your mind, and don't doubt in your heart, you will have whatever you say.   All three, mind, heart, and voice have to be in total agreement.

Confession is important because the words that are said make an impression upon your spirit to build up and reinforce your dreams and goals. Plus it releases the energy and intent of the word towards the object spoken about.   It also gives direction and permission to the Spirit.   Words are tools that help develop your desires on the inside of your spirit and when they are fully developed on the inside they will transpire on the outside.

---

[37] Ezekiel 37
[38] Proverbs 18:21

CHAPTER 20

20. Spiritual Health

Spiritual health will keep your channels of blessing open. It is important to be watchful in this area. Temptation to get off in to areas that are not spiritually healthy can block your blessings. Loneliness is a big area that can be a minefield of spiritual difficulty. In an effort to combat the pain of loneliness a person can wind up in toxic relationships, drugs, alcohol, sexual activity that is unhealthy or other behaviors that are obsessive and destructive like gambling, overspending, etc. This sort of fix for a problem only leads to more and greater problems. If someone can walk through the loneliness without the props (and maybe be lonely for a while) they will find their life much stronger and more productive in a positive way. Otherwise a lot of time is wasted on drama, tears and more unhappiness, digging them into a deeper hole. When these destructive patterns are difficult to overcome, ask the Spirit for help. If deliverance from destructive behaviors is truly desired, He will deliver. But the individual must truly want deliverance and truly repent and turn away from the area of trouble. He will set you free, if you really want to be set free.

To honor your father and mother the scripture says is "the first commandment with promise that it would be well with you and you would live long on the earth."[39] Maybe they were abusive and have no remorse for what they did, but you still forgive them. Even if you don't "feel" it you still forgive.

---

[39] Ephesians 6:2-3

That doesn't mean you have to be friends and have dinner together every Sunday. That doesn't mean you have to like them or that you agree with what they did. Just forgive even when you don't feel like it. The forgiveness will set you free from trying to deal with a bad situation and set you free from trying to right a situation that may never be straightened out. These sorts of unresolved issues can cause severe depression and other mental health issues because there is a love/hate tug of war that the emotions are engaged in. There is never any resolution and the emotions collapse in on themselves. Some things can only be changed by letting go, and forgiveness will bring you to the place of letting go. Keep forgiving until it sticks; treat them with consideration and respect, because the scripture says to for a reason, so that you will be blessed.

"Give and it shall be given unto you; good measure, pressed down, shaken together and running over."[40] If you give it has to come back because He said it works that way. What you sow, you will reap, but you can't sow with a grudging heart or a negative mindset. Bless what you give and release it with love. He is God and He owes no man anything.[41]He doesn't need your money; the silver and gold belong to Him. He is just creating an opportunity for you to be blessed. If you don't get a return on your giving He would still owe you something wouldn't He? He wouldn't be a sovereign God if he owed man something.

Idols or any representation of ungodliness, unholy or unclean things, or unholy activity will bring the spirits

---

[40] Luke 6:38
[41] Job 41:11 Living Bible

behind these things into your life and into your home. The Lord says that these things are cursed and they don't belong in your home.[42] Yes, there are some very beautiful examples of native or ethnic craftsmanship, but what do they represent? Anything that represents an idol or type of evil activity will create an open invitation for that spirit to come into your home and into your life. It will be there because you invited it in. Do you want more trouble in your life? Movies, artwork, books, the internet, furnishings and accessories in your home, tattoos, all work the same way. Be careful of what you allow in your home or in your life. Perhaps you aren't inclined to believe that it works this way, but before you judge, consider your life. The scripture says "my people are destroyed for lack of knowledge."[43]

Does it make sense that a loving Spirit would put in place commandments, codes to live by simply for punitive reasons, or just to see if you could be perfect? Would it make sense that He would be testing you just to see if you could keep all the rules? Jesus said there is none perfect, no not one. Jesus already took care of the fact that we couldn't live perfect lives. So then why are the commandments and laws there? They exist as boundary markers to tell us where the danger zones are. The Father is trying to keep your life happy and trouble free. For example, suppose you meet someone and get a knot in your stomach. Or you go somewhere and when you leave it feels like there is a layer of slimy crud all over you. That is the Spirit warning you to stay away. Listen to your intuitions, they will never lie to you and always lead you in the path of truth. Never however, confuse intuition with

---

[42] Deuteronomy 7:26
[43] Hosea 4:6 KJV

sexual attraction. They can feel similar except for the fact that one has a feeling of peace and light, and the other is pulling on you and almost forcing you. The Spirit will never compel you to do anything.

Your thoughts and desires are the seeds of what is to come into your life. The loving God put them there if they are thoughts of goodness and love. Treasure these for they are His divine will for your life. The Lord loves you, just believe, and know that He loves you.

* This book does not suggest that you throw away or discontinue any medication that you may need. When your healing arrives, then get rid of the medication.

Notes and Affirmations

Notes and Affirmations

Notes and Affirmations